Improve Presentation Skill Yourself

Er R K Shandil

ISBN 978-93-5458-520-3
© Er R K Shandil 2021
Published in India 2021 by Pencil

A brand of
One Point Six Technologies Pvt. Ltd.
123, Building J2, Shram Seva Premises,
Wadala Truck Terminal, Wadala (E)
Mumbai 400037, Maharashtra, INDIA
E connect@thepencilapp.com
W www.thepencilapp.com

DISCLAIMER: *The opinions expressed in this book are those of the authors and do not purport to reflect the views of the Publisher.*

Author biography

Ravinder Kumar Shandil, (Retd IOFS), a professional manager and academician, received his Bachelor's degree in Mechanical Engineering with Honours from Jadavpur University Kalkota and his Master's degree in Ecology and Environment from Sikkim Manipal University, Gangtok. He after serving as Principal and Lecturer in Technical institutes, he served at various positions in Indian Ordnance Factory Service for three decades and after retiring from the post of Additional General Manager in Ordnance Factories , currently residing in Shimla Hills in Himachal Pradesh, INDIA.

Now he is bringing his flavours of diverse experience to the benefit of young generation who may have been deprived of the opportunities for the lack of their presentation skill.

In this practical, easy to understand and action oriented book, "Learning/Improving Presentation Skill by yourself " will help them to apply and reveal, proven approach and methods to overcome self doubt and solve/resolve their struggle with self confidence & frustration.

Learning/Improving yourself the skill knowing that you

are good, strong & capable to attempt the skill you once thought impossible.

CONTENTS

Introduction

Most people are born with the ability to speak and converse well. But every human desires, that he should succeed. God has provided every individual with capability to achieve success. Behind every successful person there is an inherent skill which they have mastered in their early life. It is this mastery of skill which has earned them respect and place amongst the friends, relatives and all those who came in contact with them. It is their *Art of Presentation / Presentation Skill* which leaves lasting effect on all those who came into their contact. It is this skill of presentation which is responsible for their success in life.

My experience substantiates the fact that many are master in their field/ subject but they lack in their art of presentation. The majority of the talented student experience handicapped before the audience or group of people or small gatherings for lack of knowledge of how to present them.

My first exposure of speaking in front of school gathering took place when I was thirteen. It was suddenly when Head Master announced in prayer meeting that you have to address the gathering of students on current topic relating to discipline. My hands began to shake and legs wanted to tremble. Suddenly I remembered that my teacher had once explained in class how to relax by deep breathing. I at once did few deep breathing exercises and calmed myself. I did it eventually. When it was over, the students did what they were expected to do- they clapped politely as I walked off. My experience taught me that good speakers are self made and it needs mastering of the skill. However to master the skill you need to do lot of practice.

My main objective to write this book is to give you an opportunity to self learn this skill by mastering the components and develop the skill of presentation independently and with your own effort. I am sure your own effort will make you perfect in the art of presentation.

Keeping in view the objective, the process of learning the skill has been divided into following basic STEPS

STEP # 1: Recognize your potential and passion
STEP # 2: Types of presentations
STEP # 3: Presentation skill
STEP # 4: Communication
STEP # 5: Gaining control over voice
STEP #6: Developing your expressive voice
STEP #7: Body languages
STEP #8: Self image
STEP #9: Preparing the script
STEP #10: Delivering presentation
STEP #11: Salutation & Greeting

The book has been divided into ELEVEN sections, with the explanation of each having simple steps to learn the basics.

At the outset, though I want to stress that, especially in the early stage of training yourself *"21 Day Rule"* must be practiced religiously to understand its role in mastering the technique of self learning.

The *"21 Day Rule is a method of doing/saying something for 21 days, to make your something become a habit".*

Remember consistency and commitment are keys in making your 21 day rule a success, so stick at whatever you choose to do to make change happen.

Salient features of

'THINGS TO DO YOURSELF'

- You can go at your own pace.

- You think and reflect independently.

- You discover new things about yourself and improve yourself.

- You independently practice what you dreamed to do.

- You experience fun in doing yourself.

- You become self motivated and plan accordingly.

- Doing things yourself do not put pressure on you as it is your own desire to progress further.

- After doing it yourself you will feel like an entirely new person – stronger, wiser, confident and self sufficient.

- The most powerful force behind doing it yourself is that you are not scared to do things yourself because you own your opinion and you yourself have decided to do it yourself.

- You do not need any body's permission to do it.

- In doing yourself you work hard for yourself and this will sharpen your creative ability.

- Doing it yourself and learning a new skill will remind/apprise you just how smart and capable you really are.

Hence it is imperative to spend time on learning art of presentation/Presentation Skill daily, as much as you can afford to master it. My advice is not to procrastinate if you want success in life.

God's wishes are with you for your new journey of learning the ***Art of Presentation/Presentation Skill***

Step-1
Recognize Your Potential And Passion

ESTABLISHING YOUR POTENTIAL AND PASSION

Identifying your potential in life is important to your overall development and happiness. Knowing what you are good at and what you want to do in life will make your life more satisfying and fulfilling.

Now the question arises what you love to do. It means what is your passion. Your passion is a specific area which will enhance your ability to achieve in related activity. But remember, your passion can come out only when you have skill to present it and to present it; you need to know the art of presentation. Hence you have to practice the skill to present yourself.

Before knowing anything else, you need to know yourself first. You need to know your weaknesses, strengths, beliefs and desires. All your weaknesses, strengths, beliefs and desires are reflected by your emotions. So to control your emotions you have to be self-aware. The most important thing of a leader is the ability to monitor his own emotions and reactions. Learning how to control your emotions and reactions might not be so easy, but if you sincerely practice the exercises given in this book will surely help you to develop the skill of controlling the emotions and reactions. Those who proactively obtain new skill (skill of presentation) have the highest potential to succeed. *"New skill is acquired if you have ability to change, adapt and evolve yourself before it is really required".*

Each emotion creates a specific combination of facial expression, body language and other physiological cues such as heart beat or sweating of palms. So to say, each emotion may be represented by a whole range of reactions in the brain and the body. Emotions can be seen in the forms of *love, hate, nervousness, frustration, openness, defensiveness, cooperation and confidence.*

Before dealing with our emotions, we must understand the **potential**. As per Wikipedia, *the potential generally refers to a currently unrealized ability and human potential is the capacity for human to improve themselves through studying, training and practice, to reach the limit of their ability to develop aptitudes and skills.*

If you aspire to search for, how to identify your potential, you will find enormous articles on the subject suggesting ways to reach the highest potential. Now the question arose about the origin of *human potential.*

If you happen to study the evolution theory, one thing is very clear that evolution process is a continuous and we can find that everything in nature is continuously evolving. All plants, animal and all living creatures (including human beings) on earth, either on land or in water are in the process of evolution. If you closely study one specie i.e., human beings you will notice that human beings are continuously is in the process of evolution. *The force which is causing evolution is the inherent potential of every human being.*

Newly born child (material taken from earth) evolve into adolescent boy, adolescent boy into fully grown man, man into old man and ultimately evolve back to earth on death. This process of evolution occurs to every human being in different surroundings and environment. Hence, this human potential is the inherent capacity of human to improve them unconsciously. As the process of evolution is occurring unconsciously the human are not aware of this inherent potential. This inherent potential of man is to be recognized and to be cultivated for our growth. *Awareness is the state of being aware, or having knowledge of something.*Now you are aware of your inherent potential. Hence you can effectively control your emotions. All the philosophers, inventors, scholars, saints and all those admired by millions were aware of this inherent potential and utilized this awareness to reach highest place in life.

The most important factor which is evident here is that life starts when you start breathing and ends when you stop breathing but this happens under the control of inherent potential. Hence it is evident here that the control of breathing can regulate human potential.

We all know that we breathe air, contain 78% of Nitrogen and 21% of Oxygen and traces of other gases. When we inhale (breathe-in), air enters our lungs and oxygen from the air moves from your lungs to your blood. At the same time, carbon-dioxide a waste gas, moves from your blood to the lungs and is exhaled (breathe-out). Our Brain control our breathing rate (how fast or slow we breathe), by sensing our body's need for oxygen and its need to get rid of carbon-dioxide.

There are three major organs which consumes the most oxygen. Liver consumes 20%, Brain consumes 18% and Heart consumes 12%. Since the brain consumption of oxygen fluctuates as compared to other organs, the average consumption of oxygen universally accepted is 20%. Beside oxygen, brain also uses more energy than any other human organ. It consumes 20% of the Total Energy produced in the body.

As mentioned earlier that each emotions are represented by the range of reactions in brain and the body, we need to keep our brain active by supply of sufficient oxygen so that it can proactively handle the emotions. This can be effectively done through Deep Breathing exercises. Deep breathing can help our lungs to reach full capacity. Deep breathing helps us to relax and reduce tension and anxiety. To our surprise the human beings take in about 550 liters of pure Oxygen per day to maintain healthy body. This can be effectively done through Deep Breathing Exercises.

THINGS TO DO YOURSELF

1. Passion: Anything you love to do is passion. Your passion may be anything. Example-Singing, Gardening, Playing game, reading books, Helping people, Writing, Dancing, etc.

2. Apply 'Rule-21' : Work on your passion for 21 days so that it becomes your habit.

3. Human Potential: is the capacity of human to improve through studying, training and practice. Nourish your passion by utilizing your inherent potential. Apply 'Rule-21'

4. Strengthen your Brain Capability; Brain uses 20% of Oxygen and 20% of Energy of your body. Strengthen its capability by Deep breathing. 'Apply Rule-21' this will automatically control your emotions.

Step - 2 Types Of Presentation

FIVE TYPES OF PRESENTATION

You had been spending an enormous amount of time and energy on what you think you won't be able to do. But the "Things To Do yourself" has helped you to find out your *Passion*("The thing which you love to do") and motivated you to prepare yourself. The fear factor of failure, the uncertainty and anxiety has now taken the back seat in your mind.

Once you get rid of these feelings, you have now new approach to allow you to focus on what you want to do. You may be in dilemma to learn the skill of presentation. Before you learn the art of presentation, you need to know little about the type of presentations. Presentations have different forms and have variety of purpose depending upon the needs. There are five types of well established forms/ types of presentations.

1. SALE PRESENTATION:- The sales presentation involves selling and marketing. It may promote products, service and benefits. Here you speak to people about the product and put up a show, so you become showman. Your objective here is to sell and at the end of your presentation people come up to you and say, thank you, it was very interesting.

2. EDUCATIONAL PRESENTATION:- In this presentation your objective is to teach. It includes training programs and class lectures. This needs a particular skill. In class room you need audience participation. This is achieved by asking questions, not commenting on answers and in the end gives correct answer. Educational presentation must be practical. The more you are practical, it is easier for the audience to understand and remember. When you are teaching it is important to repeat the concept a number of times. The more you say the more the audience will remember.

3. MOTIVATIONAL PRESENTATION;- It includes the range of presentation such as political, annual sales, sermons, motivational talks. Objective of this presentation is to excite the audience, inspire and spur them into action. The more you exaggerate your presentation the more successful it will be.

4. FACTUAL PRESENTATION:- Factual presentation is generally done to merely present factual information. Factual information may be reports, data, budgets or financial status. The intention of the presentation is to give you facts so that the audience can follow and comprehend. In this presentation you take the help of visual supports such as overhead slides or handouts.

5. FORMAL PRESENTATION:- The formal presentation is the presentation delivered in the formal setting. Formal setting may be board

meeting, interview, retirement party, particular problem solving meeting, reception and small group meeting. So the formal presentation is basically the presentation where ideas are effectively presented to the individual or group of people suited to the needs of audience. Hence this presentation can be based upon requirement of audience needs. The presentation in formal setting such as dinner speech, reception, retirement speech and interview does not require the help of visual support. Whereas the other formal setting such as presentation to Board meeting, seminars and small group meetings require the help of visual supports. These supports may be in the form of overheads, slides or handouts. In the Formal meeting presentation you either talk about someone or on the subject of interest of audience, where you have to arouse their feelings. The easiest way to create feeling is with your voice and body language. Ninety percent of effect on audience comes from your voice and body language.

Step - 3
Presentation Skill

STRUCTURE OF YOUR PRESENTATION

The main aim of writing this book is to learn the presentation skill using our inherent potential. The presentation skill covers a variety of areas such as the Structure of your presentation, design of slides and tone of your voice and Body language you convey. This can be achieved through learning the further details of Formal Presentation and to develop the skill we need to follow certain established norms.

It is important to create a structure that helps your audience to understand your message. If the presentation is not organized, your listeners have to search for the message you want to convey. If you force them to search the message, you will lose your audience attention. Structure is important because a well organized presentation creates an impression that you know what you are talking about- you will gain the audience trust. The structure will not only make you comfortable but also help you to pre- assess the knowledge and need of your audience so that you are delivering the *the right presentation to the right audience*.

DESIGN OF SLIDES

1. 10-20-30 Rule of Power Point Presentation:-This represent the concise and visibility of your presentation.

*   *10- Slides:* By limiting to only 10-slides, you will manage the learning load on your audience. This will help the audience to follow your flow of presentation and also help you to choose to show on slides only what's important.

*   *20- Minutes:-* Always limit your presentation time to 20- minutes only. This will help you leave out unnecessary details and focus on the important material that will convey your message. Even if your session has been allotted with more time, you can devote the remaining time to discussion & questions to involve your audience in presentation.

*   *30- Font Size:-* Depending upon the room & screen size, most audience will be able to see text that are at least 30- Size Font. This font size has been mostly accepted on the basis that anything you show must be visible to everybody in attendance, especially those in the back seat. Keep also in

mind that these rules vary depending on the situation.

1. *6X6 Rule:-* Another rule is 6X6 which limits any text to 6 words per line and 6 lines per slide. Similar to 10-20-30 rule, it focuses on readability and clarity. Too much text can be tiring for audience to read. The audience is there to listen and watch you, not read your slides.

TONE OF YOU'RE VOICE

When you make a presentation to the group of people, it is important to have authoritative and appealing tone of your voice. The tone of your voice indicates a particular feeling. It may be joyful, serious, humorous, sad, threatening, formal, informal, pessimistic or optimistic. There are various ways to improve your vocal voice and it will be separately dealt in forthcoming chapter in detail.

NON VERBAL SIGNALS

Body Language is non-verbal signal that we use to communicate in presentation. So the body language is a mixture of gestures, postures, facial expressions, eye contact, touch, and voice and body movement. When your non-verbal signals match up the words you are saying, they increase trust, clarity and rapport. When they do not match with your saying, it generates tension, mistrust and confusion in audience. There are various ways to improve your Body Language and it will be separately dealt in forthcoming chapter in detail.

THINGS TO DO YOURSELF

- Types of Presentation:- Read the chapter number of times till you are familiar with types of presentations.- memorize them

- Design your Presentation:- Any conversation with your dear you had in the past be prepared on Power Point Presentation in format showing Structure, 10-20-30 Rule, 6X6 Rule.- Remember they are very important norms- Memorize them.

Step - 4
Communication

UNDERSTANDING COMMUNICATION PROCESS

Your inherent potential has motivated you and now you want to be better speaker. Not only better but you want to be great and powerful speaker. What do you have to do to be so? You must be looking for the answer. The answer is 'how to communicate'. Communication is two way process. Communication is the act of conveying meaning from one entity or group to another through the use of mutually understood signs, symbols and semiotic rules. Or in simple words the communication is simply the act of transferring information from one place, person or group to another. Every communication involves at least one sender, a message and a recipient. When we meet someone face to face, we have three 'V' to communicate.

- *VERBAL* (What we say)

- *VOCAL*   (How we say)

- *VISUAL*   (How we look)

In any conversation, or in workshop or in public speaking we often communicate in 3 'V'. Research has shown that these three elements in a message have following proportions.

- The Verbal   -   7%

- The Vocal   - 38%

- The Visual   - 55%

In general, it is not just what we say, but how we say and how we look when we say.

All the above mentioned proportion work in combination with each other and not independently. In other words, it does not mean that you look good, have a great voice and talk utter rubbish and get away with because your content is 7% while everything else adds up to 93%. The verbal, vocal and visual always work together. If you take away, one of the 3 'V', the effect is lost and your presentation loses the impact.

If you want your message to get across effectively, you need a good focused script- this is verbal (what you say), but the delivery relies on the enthusiasm in your voice- this is vocal (how we sound) and energy and sincerity of your face and body language- visual (how we look). Remember when you give a presentation, you are giving a performance and this performance if is based upon 3'V' of communication, it will surely have impact on the senses of the audience and they will feel involved.

How to improve your communication through verbal, vocal and visual, in-depth understanding of these will be done in forthcoming chapters.

THINGS TO DO YOURSELF

1. While in conversation with your friends try to watch your verbal, vocal and visual activities.

Repeat this review with others such as teachers, parents or in small group of friends.

2. Watch and observe others how they use 3 "V". Observe how they sound, how they look and how they use their body language while discussing the topic.

Step - 5 Gaining Cantrol Over Voice

EMPOWERING YOUR VOICE

In human, voice is produced by the Voice Box (larynx) present in the upper part of human body, i.e. near the upper end of the wind pipe. When human speaks, the muscle present in the Voice Box (larynx) gets stretched and opening becomes narrow. When the air is made to pass through this narrow passage the vocal cord vibrate and produce sound. Human beings are capable of regulating/ control the stretching of the muscle in voice box, are the reason why human voice has different pitches.

Voice of children, men and women are different because they have different length of vocal cord. The vocal cord in women is about 15 mm long; in men vocal cord is about 20 mm long and in children have very short vocal cord.

Before we take up the empowering of voice we must understand the mechanism involved in it. In producing the speech following three crucial mechanisms are involved.

- Energy comes from the air supplied by the lungs.

- The vocal folds produce sound at the sound box (larynx).

- The sound is then filtered or shaped by the articulators.

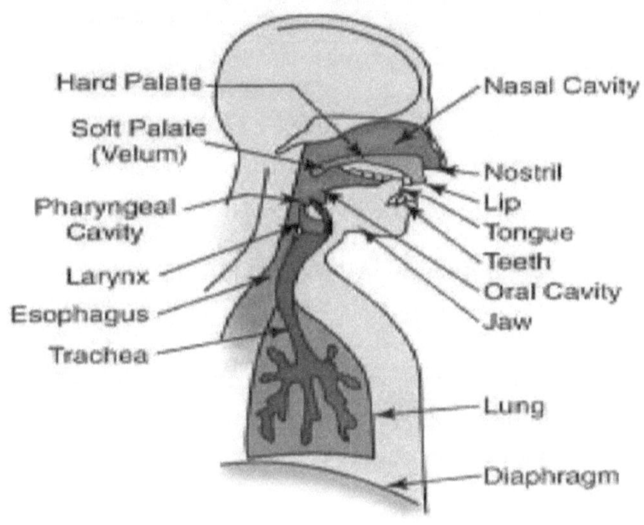

We have already gained little knowledge about first two, but we must know about the third aspect i.e. articulators. Following different parts are called articulators.

- The tube (pharynx) which is above the sound box (larynx). It is about 7 cm long in women and 8 cm in men and at its top end it is divided into two parts, one part is the back of mouth and other being the beginning of way through the nasal cavity.

- Soft Palate: - allows the air to pass through the nose and through the mouth.

- Hard Palate: is often called the 'roof of the mouth'. You can feel its smooth curved surface with your tongue.

- Alveolar ridge: -- Ridge / place between your front teeth and hard palate.

- Tongue; - a very important articulator and it can be moved into many different places and different shapes.

- Teeth (upper & lower); - are in the front of mouth.

- Lips: - very important in speech, they can be pressed together, brought into contact with teeth and can be rounded.

From the above it is evident that producing sounds while speaking, this crucial mechanism plays a very important role. Now it is very clear that vibration is produced on the outflow of breath. Therefore, breathing is the basis of voice. It is the energy of the lungs which causes the air to flow. It is this energy which propels the voice forward. The greater the energy, the stronger the flow of air, better the sound will be.

So learning, how to improve your breathing is the first step in gaining control over your voice. Before we learn to improve the speech, it is pertinent to mention here that in order to keep the crucial mechanism to be active during the speech; you need to do following two things.

- Keep the upper portion above Voice Box (including voice box) lubricated by drinking water, before, in-between /during and at the end of the presentation so that you do not produce hoarse sound.

- Keep the lower portion below voice box fully filled up with air because 20% of Oxygen is consumed by Brain during presentation and rest of air your lungs require to send it through voice box for speaking. Hence deep breathing is a must.

DEEP BREATHING EXCERCISES.

There are few deep breathing exercises which will improve the capacity of your lungs to retain more air so that you gain skill in presentation.

1. Lip Breathing: How to do it.

- Relax your neck and shoulder.

- Keep your mouth closed and inhale through your nose for 3 counts.

- Curve your lips as you are going to whistle.

- Exhale slowly by blowing air through the curved lips for count of 5.

- Repeat 4-5 times.

2. Diaphragmatic Breathing: How to do it.

- Lie down on your back with knee slightly bent and keep pillow under your head.

- Keep one hand on your upper chest and other hand below your rib cage, so that you can feel the movement of diaphragm.

- Slowly inhale through your nose, and feel as if your stomach is pressing into your hand.

- Exhale through your lips.

- Repeat number of times.

3. Alternate Nostril Breathing: This breathing is also known as Nadi Shodhna Pranayam in Sanskrit. This is best exercise for relaxation. It is to be practiced on an empty stomach. How to do it.

- Choose a comfortable position.

- Bring your hand up in front of your face and press your thumb on the outside of one nostril.

- Inhale deeply through your open nostril.

- At the peak of your inhalation, release your thumb.

- Press your ring finger on the outside of your other nostril, and exhale.

- Continue this pattern for 3-4 times, beginning with same nostril and ending with other.

- Now reverse the pattern to start with other nostril and ending with first nostril.

- Spend equal amounts of time inhaling and exhaling through both nostrils.

4. Relaxing Breath. This breathing exercise has its root in yoga's pranayama which help people to learn how to gain control over their breath. How to do it.

- Begin by sitting or lying down in comfortable position.

- Your eyes can be open or closed.

- Press the tip of your tongue to the roof of your mouth.

- Slightly open your mouth and exhale until you reach the bottom of your breath.

- Close your mouth and quietly inhale through your nose for 4 counts.

- Then hold your breath for 7 counts.

- Finally, exhale very slowly so that it takes a total of 8 counts to return to the bottom of your breath.

- Repeat for 4 full breath.

- Over a passage of time increase to work your ways to 8 full breath.

Now remember the time when you had to speak in front of small gathering or while at interview, you feel your chest tight, your heart is pounding, your mouth go dry and words stick to your throat. This happens because your rhythm of breathing has disrupted. That means you do not breathe properly.

The correct method of breathing is called inter costal diaphragmatic breathing, because the muscles that used are intercostals muscles (situated between ribs) and the diaphragm (a large muscle situated at the base of the ribs). In other words your lungs are surrounded by the rib cage in the front and back, and the diaphragm at the bottom. For lungs to expand, both the ribs cage and the diaphragm have to move. During breathing, air is taken in, the muscle automatically contract, lifting the rib cage out, at the same time, the diaphragm moves downward. Even if you tense up the inhalation process is involuntary, means that you cannot stop breathing.

During exhalation process, the reverse happens. The ribs moves inward and the abdominal organs exert an upward pressure so that the diaphragm can move upward to its relaxed position. This movement of diaphragm is gradual and provides study flow of air for the purpose of speech.

Your voice is the barometer of your emotions. The listener can observe your emotions in the form of fear, impatience and anxiety. This is due to the abnormal muscular activity (the abdominal organ which exerts upward pressure) that takes place when you create voice. When you are angry or nervous, your voice tense up easily. So in order to control your emotion you should learn to control your abnormal muscular activity. You can easily train your voice to do what you want because muscles can be trained. So it is must to learn, how to control this muscular activity. This muscular activity can be easily controlled by following ways.

- Breathe Out:- As explained earlier that the upward movement of diaphragm should be gradual and provide steady flow of air for the purpose of speech, but when you are tense up this upward flow of diaphragm is restricted due to muscular tension. So in order to relax the muscle you must breathe out. We know that breathing is basis of relaxation, production of voice and energy to the voice. But when you are tense up you hold your breath. That is why we feel as though we are running short of air. Hence the only way to release your tension is to breathe out.

- Breathing Exercises:- If the lungs capacity is inadequate to maintain steady flow of air through the voice box, the lungs capacity needs improvement. The capacity of lungs can be increased by breathing exercises already explained. You can select one of the above mentioned exercises. Make it a point that you practice the breathing exercise every day at least 3-4 times.

THINGS TO DO YOURSELF

- Breathing Exercises:- You can select one of the exercise which you feel most adoptable to you and practice sincerely every day at least for a duration of 5-6 minutes.

- Breathing Out:- After breathing exercises make it a point to do breathing out exercise.

RESONANCE

Till now we have understood the two critical mechanisms responsible for producing the voice. The third mechanism responsible for amplification of sound needs our attention.

In simplest way the resonance is defined as the amplification of sound. Good resonance will produce excellent tone and forward projection of voice. Therefore it is necessary to improve your resonance because the sound when produced by vibration of vocal cord is very feeble. Hence you need to amplify it so that it is audible to others. To gain control over your voice you need to develop your resonance. Before we learn about resonance, we must understand the mechanism behind sound production.

In order to produce sound we need three things.

- An instrument that can vibrate (Voice Box)

- Something to make the vibration (An Activator)

- An amplification Chamber. (Resonator and Articulator)

The rapid pulses of air created (in the Voice Box) by the repeat vibratory cycles produces 'voiced sound' which is a 'buzz sound', which then is amplified by resonators and articulators, producing the sound 'as we know it'

The vocal cord vibrates as follows, and we recognize them as:

- 110 cycles/sec ---- Lower pitch ----- Men voice

- 180-220 cycles/sec-Medium pitch-Women voice

- 300 cycles/sec – Higher pitch---Children voice

Voice resonance is often referred to as the quality of someone's voice. Your voice may be deep, rich and full or it may be high, sharp and penetrating. As it has been stated earlier, sound is created by the speed and vibration of air through the vocal cord. The voice resonance is determined by the size of the cavity through which the air vibration takes place. This cavity is found in our throat, mouth and nasal passage. The differences in sizes of our physical cavity are the reason why we have different voices. When you have a cold and your nasal passage is blocked, your voice does not resonate well. That is why the people sound funny when they are sick.

We know that hard surface bounce off the sound with clarity, while the soft surface absorbs the sound. Now let us find the surface where we can make the sound bounce off with clarity. This can be done by you by using your tongue. By running your tongue, you find that top of your teeth (alveolar) and hard palate (the roof of your mouth) are only two surfaces, which are hard. So the resonance will occur in the front of the face (top of your teeth and the roof of your mouth) only.

Hence by practicing to use hard surfaces you may

develop deep, rich and full voice. In addition the good resonance is also dependent on strong flow of air. You can improve your resonance by combining the pushing the sound forward and breathing exercises.

- Exercise- I: -- Take a deep breath while silently counting 4 or more. Hold deep breath for the same count. Then breath out and as you exhale make sound of mm, mm, mm,. Try to push the sound forward as much as possible. Always concentrate on pushing the sound forward and keep the sound going as long as you feel you have air. Repeat ten times or more.

- Exercise-II:- Take a deep breath. Breath out, and as you do so make sound mmm mah . Open your mouth as wide as you can for mah sound and stretch it out as long as you can. Repeat ten times or more.

These two basic exercises will help you to improve to your resonance. You should spend at least ten minutes per day doing these exercises so that you develop great voice.

THINGS TO DO YOURSELF

Exercise- I: Ten times a day.
Exercise- II: Ten times a day.

These two exercises may appear very simple and dull but they are very effective. Do not ignore them.

ARTICULATION

Articulation is the ability to physically move the tongue, lips, teeth and jaws to produce the range of speech sound of words and sentences which are clear and can be easily understood by others. It is required to express the basic needs to others. Strong spoken articulation is often associated with being more intelligent and more capable of projecting yourself.

There are six simple ways to become more articulate in your personal and professional life.

1. Listen to yourself:- Before implementing the corrective steps you must record how you participate in conversation. Generally people hate their own sound/voice. This is not a proper attitude. Remember your own voice is unique, because others want to listen and have conversation with you. Listening to your own voice can help you to know your run-on sentences, which you need to fix. Run-on defect can be found out only when you listen to your voice.

2. Don't be afraid to pronounce:- If you afraid to pronounce the word you mumble. Get away the problem of mumbling by practicing the pronouncing of word again and again. At last you

will perfect it. Another way is to practice slow speaking so that you gain confidence to stop mumbling. Slow speaking also gives more time to audience to understand your thoughts. So, slightly slow your speed, your mumbling will die out.

3. Keep it Simple: - If you have lot to say, you should use simple structure sentences while speaking. Long sentences will lose the attention of the audience and you may even forget what you wanted to say in the first place.

4. Do not use fillers: - Do not use filler words such as 'um' 'uh' and 'like'. These words indicate to your audience that you are unsure of your direction. You can replace fillers by 'Let's move on to' or 'Another important consideration'.

5. Pay attention to your audience: - This is the most important tip. Your audience plays a consistent role in how you speak. Keep listeners interested in what you say. You can vary your pitch high or low in your voice in order to keep your audience interested. This is how you can also learn to become more articulate. Practice for high and low and long and short, pitches with your normal/ natural flow of speech at least for 5-10 minutes per day. It should be done consciously.

6. Voice Projection: - You should be capable of projecting of your voice with enough energy or intensity so that anyone who is 8-10 feet away can clearly understand you. Practice talking at this intensity so that they can follow what you are

saying, thereby drawing favourable attention to yourself.

THINGS TO DO YOURSELF

1. Listen to your own voice:- Using your mobile, listen to your voice number of times so that you are familiar with your voice and you start loving your voice.

2. Let your Speech be heard at least 10 ft away:-Use your mobile to record your voice at a distance of 5-7 ft away and look for its clarity. Increase your pitch so that it is clearly audible at 10 ft distance. Practice till there is clarity in words and sentences.

3. Record your Conversation:- Observe the pattern of your recorded conversation. Learn to deliver small sentences instead of long sentences. This will empower your speech.

4. Avoid Fillers:- Record your voice and search for the fillers. Try to replace your fillers by 'Let us move on' etc.

Step - 6
Developing An Expressive Voice

HOW TO PRACTICE EXPRESSIVE VOICE

Up till now you have understood that the foundation of well modulated voice is deep breathing, forward resonance and ability to physically move the tongue, lips, teeth and jaws (articulators). Now you are mentally prepared to develop a most expressive voice. The only way to develop a vibrant well modulated voice with excellent tone is to practice using different tones and expressions. Now the question will arise in your mind is *"How to practice"*.

You may remember when you first learned how to drive? How awkward it was and how difficult you felt learning. Then when you mastered the method, you became so proficient in driving that you are called expert. This is a natural process we go through such experience whenever we learn new skill.

Now you should know what practice you do to make your voice *'Expressive'*. Reading aloud is the only way to make your voice expressive. So to practice reading aloud is the best thing. You will find pleasure that more you read aloud, the better your voice will be. If you read aloud daily, you will find that you comfortable with your own sound and quality of your voice will improve.

Reading aloud will help you gaining following advantages.

- It brings clarity to your voice.

- It improves pronunciation.

- It acts as a practice ground for other components of speech.

- It boasts confidence and reduces hesitation.

- It will make you understand punctuation. (to pause at comma, full stop)

While reading aloud, following rules must be followed so that your voice contain good expression and is well projected.

Rule- 1:-   Always read to someone or something at the opposite end of the room.

Remember if you read aloud to yourself, it will not project and you defeat the objective of the exercise. But if you read aloud to someone at the opposite end of the room, you will automatically speak in a louder/stronger voice because your intention is to be heard clearly and properly at the other end. This will slow down your speaking speed and you will learn to pause during speaking.

Rule- 2 :-- Reading material should be different.

1. <u>Reading Newspaper Story</u>:- It will help to learn how to make the opportunities interesting. Your speed and pauses will automatically vary.

2. <u>Novel Reading</u>:- It will help you to learn how to express sadness, joy or smile while reading the context.

3. <u>Advertisement Reading</u>:- It will help you to learn how to be expressive so that you achieve the objective of selling and pursuing others to buy your product.

4. <u>Poetry Reading</u>:- To read poetry you need to first understand the mood of the poetry, it is trying to create.

So it is recommended that you should start with reading newspaper, novels and advertisement and then gradually if you feel go for poetry.

Rule 3; Pause where it makes sense to pause:-

Remember that spoken words are different from written script. While reading the written script aloud, it not necessary to pause at comma. Comma has been placed due to grammatical reason. So you should pause where it makes sense. Before reading aloud, mark the pauses with slash (/). The pauses are essential to allow your audience to digest the message. Take your time at pauses remembering that you are speaking to someone who is at the opposite end of the room.

Rule-4:-- Start with short paragraph at the beginning.

It is beneficial to read short paragraphs- say ten to

fifteen lines to start with. The reason for the advice for short paragraphs is that you will find it difficult to sustain an expressive voice over a long period of time.

IMPORTANT NOTE

Reading aloud will help you to improve your voice in a relatively short time. You will learn how to place more emphasis on particular word and less on others. Your rhythm of the language will improve and in addition you will improve the use of pauses and stress. Your pitch will also improve. All desired requirement for developing your voice are met by reading aloud.

THINGS TO DO YOURSELF

Rule-1. Repeat this practice daily at least 2-4 times
Rule-2. While practicing rule-1 exercises, change
        reading material daily.
Rule-3. Apply Rule-3 (pauses) while practicing
        Rule-1.
Rule-4. Apply Rule-4 while practicing Rule-1.
       Repeat this at rule-1 for minimum of 4-6 times.

Step - 7 Body Language

Non Verbal Signals of Body

Body languages are the unspoken elements of our communication that reveal our true feelings and emotions. Our basic emotional body language is natural. You must have seen newly born baby smiling. No one teaches him. The small babies gurgle with delight when they are happy and make faces and cry when they are unhappy. Body language, in itself, is very fascinating. We reveal our feeling by changing the various parts of our body including facial expressions. When we are angry, certain facial muscles automatically come into play and change the expression of our face, eyes and around mouth. When our body muscles tense up, we store our strength, to fight it back. Without body language our message carries no weight.

Body language is natural. We learn few body languages from the culture we move around and in addition we also adopt some from immediate environment. Human beings are highly visual creative on earth, who is easily influenced by what we see and feel.

You can easily judge people from their body language, whether they support your message or distract from it. Therefore the correct body language is extremely important to the presentation.

There is an old saying, "Action speaks louder than words". Our body posture, along with its movement and placement of different body parts, plays an important role in letting out our feelings and emotions, even if we do not display the emotions voluntarily. Hence correct body language is extremely important to your presentation. The last thing you want as a speaker is that your emotion need not fight against your body language. A nervous smile, shaky hands, incorrect head position, a slight clinching of the fists—all can prevent you from expressive presentation.

The last part of your presentation technique which requires your attention is to master the visual communication which represents 55% of your presentation. Visuals are everything your audience sees - the podium area, you and what you are wearing and any other visual aids. So you must perfect your body language. It is very easy to learn correct body language which will enhance your image. The little knowledge of body language can change your image from mediocre to magnificent. You can accomplish this by learning how to manage six areas of body language. They are

- HANDS AND GESTURE

- POSTURE

- HEAD POSITION

- LEG AND FEET POSITION

- EYE CONTACT

- FACIAL EXPRESSION

HAND POSITION

Among all species, our human hands are unique. Human hand can paint, play the instrument, write, scratch, pinch, punch, poke, hold and mold the world around us. Most of the people do not know about the body language of our hand beside this they would not be able to describe what their hand can reveal.

The most comfortable position of your hand while delivering a presentation is in the area around your belly button, with your elbows relaxed against your sides. When you are in party you never feel difficulties with your hands, because at party we usually hold our drink or plate of food around our waist area because it is comfortable. You need to practice this hands position before any presentation.

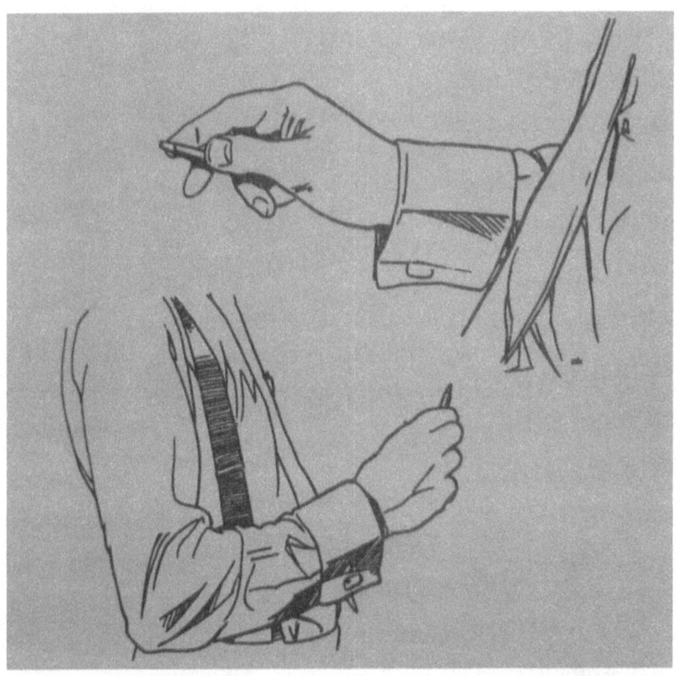

How it is to done. You can do by holding a pen or pencil at waist area as if you are holding a glass or food plate, whenever you get up from your chair to walk anywhere, take a pen. When you stand and talk to a colleague at the office, hold on to pen. But do not play with pen. Do not twist it around nor pull the cap off. The pen position teaches you how to place your hand naturally.

Once you have learned to place your hand and practiced a lot, you can stop using pen or pencil. Whenever again you find discomfort with your hand, you practice with pen.

GESTURE

Before we discuss about hand gesture, there is scientific research about hand gestures, which is as follows:-

- You are born to speak with your hands.

- Hand gesture make people listen to you.

- Hand gesture comes to you naturally.

- Gesturing helps you to access memory.

- Hand gestures help you to understand more.

It is a fact that hand gestures is natural part of our speech. Again, it is fact that the correct use of hand movement adds poise and confidence to the way you appear when presenting in front of audience. Hand movement help create an interest in audience.

The first step in learning how to gesture is to know where your hand should be when they are still. As we have learnt above it is around your belly button area. Because gesture is natural and differs in every individual, so you will observe people using their gesture differently. Following drills will help you to learn, how to move your hands naturally.

DRILL- 1 :

- Pick up a pen,

- Allow your arm and hands fall straight down to the sides of your body,

- Go and ask your colleagues something, as you do so, bring your hands up to belly button area.

- Do this exercise number of times daily.

- Practice till it becomes your habit

DRILL-2:

- Easiest way to practice for your hands position is to have conversation with someone while holding pen or pencil at belly button area.

- Practice till it becomes your habit

DRILL-3:

- Whenever you get a chance, walk around the office or home while holding pen or pencil, letting your arms sway as you walk.

- Practice till it becomes your habit.

All the above mentioned drill teaches you hand movements and with practice it will become your natural habit. It does not matter if this takes you a month or a year to learn. Remember there should not be a time limit to acquire the skill. Develop your own expressive movement of hands, so that it enhances your image.

POSTURE

Posture is the way that a person looks, sits, stands, walks etc. When you use good posture, your muscles and other body structure parts function properly and you do not feel any joint stress. Good posture is the proper alignment of your body, when standing, walking or sitting. Many of us spend lot of time sitting either at work, at school, or at home. So it becomes necessary to sit properly so that other body structure parts are not unnecessarily stressed. To avoid the unnecessary stress you need to take frequent breaks. Following are few actions you need to take to improve your posture when sitting.

- Switch sitting position frequently.

- Take brief walks – around your office

    -- around your home

- Stretch your muscles gently- This should be done so often, so that your muscles release tension.

- Relax your shoulders.

- Make sure that your back is fully supported. Use back rest or pillow to support your backbone, so that it is always straight.

- Make sure your feet touch the ground or footrest.

Following are few actions you need to take to improve your posture when standing.

- Always stand straight and upright.

- Pull your stomach in.

- Keep your head level straight- Do not look up or down

- Keep your feet about shoulder width apart.

HEAD POSITION

While sitting or standing your head position must be straight. Your head will be always straight if your chin forms imaginary upside down letter "L" If it is too high or too low, the inverted "L" won't form correctly. If you keep your chin too high you look arrogant/aloof.

LEG AND FEET POSITION

The leg and feet position differ for men and women, therefore it need separate consideration.

MEN:- Man should space their feet about shoulder width

apart. Or to say men should stand their feet hip wide and facing forward. The weight should be evenly distributed on and along both feet. If you place your weight on one foot, you will sway slightly from side to side. A firm standing conveys strength. Do not move your feet without reason. You should walk only when it is required. For perfect leg and feet position you should avoid following things.

- You should avoid crossing one foot over the other.

- Do not tap your foot and make noise. It is distracting.

- Do not shuffle in a small circle.

WOMEN:- Women should not stand their feet hip wide. Their feet should be about 2 to 2 ½ inches apart. They're both feet should be either facing forward or one foot forward and other slightly to the side. Your weight should be evenly distributed on both feet, as this will prevent you from swaying.

EYE CONTACT

Of course, you do not have to spend your entire presentation staring into the eyes of your audience. Looking up, looking around the room or looking away from your audience is absolutely fine. But make sure that you are meeting their eyes for most of your presentation. Keep in mind that your eye contact should be so frequent that it appears as though you are talking to them and not talking at them.

You cannot talk to people effectively if you do not look at them and have an eye contact. Indirect eye contact makes your delivery insincere. Remember that the eye contact is an extraordinary power of the presenter due to following reasons.

- Eye Contact with audience keeps you focused with them.

- Looking into eyes is scary and hard but it develops bonding with them.

FACIAL EXPRESSION

Your facial expression is the most expressive part of your body language. Our face has 42 muscles which can be molded to show smile, frown, show concern, anger, confidence, sympathy, nervousness, fatigue, etc. Whatever you feel can be shown on the face. Other few facial expressions may be making eye contact, eye rolling, bored or interested appearance.

Human face has the most complex series of muscles. As pointed out above there are 42 individual facial muscles responsible for making different expressions. So we should learn to use these muscles and develop the following expressive abilities.

- Smile when it is appropriate.

- Look serious when it is appropriate.

- Look concerned when it is appropriate.

- Eye contact when it is appropriate.

- Learn to match your eye contact with facial expression.

The most expressive face is when you are relaxed. Be aware of your face when you are relaxed. Watch yourself closely in mirror when smiling, serious and concerned, and objectively see your expressions. All the above mentioned expressions you should do by practicing in front of mirror while saying different things. Do it again and again and watch your face while you say things. This will help you to improve your facial expression.

Step - 8
Enhancing Your image

Self image

We all struggle with our poor self image. It is because that we compare our self with others. Before we enhance our image we should have our own introspection.

1. Who are you:- Take some time to know yourself by highlighting your qualities, value and recognize any thing that you see about yourself. Remember you have inherent potential and passion. Recognize your passion and hence improve your image in that direction.

2. Why you want to change:- It is only your inherent potential which guides us and develop new skill because of our own capability to change.

3. Create New Image;-- You should redefine yourself and knowing your capabilities, you should create your new image and work sincerely to make it your new habit and then deal with new people and new situation.

4. Do not put yourself Down:-- Never put yourself down in front of others. By putting yourself down in front of others, you are basically telling them, you do not value yourself. Do not allow them to think in this way.

5. Visualization;-- Visualize your new image best suited to you. Work on it sincerely.

In addition to above introspection, we need to know few dimensions which reflect our image.

1. Physical Dimension: Know and evaluate your personal appearance.

2. Personality Dimension: Evaluate and know your thoughts, feeling and behavior which distinguishes you from others individual personality.

3. Intelligence Dimension: It is the ability to understand, learn and think. You are aware of the fact that you are unique and you have the capability of solving the problem and take correct decision because you have inherent potential.

4. Skill Dimension: Skill defines both the work itself and the qualification you need to successfully perform the work. So we need to improve social and technical skills performance.

The first impression that you make on people, the image they have of you, is made in first sixty second and that impression is lasting one. The above mentioned traits of your personality (Physical, Personality and Intelligence and Skill dimensions) are observed by audience in first sixty seconds.

(Note: Here we shall be touching only self image related to your appearance only)

Very often you have looked at someone and you have formed your opinion about him without even talking to him. You have formed about him the impression within first sixty seconds.

So when you make a presentation, it is essential to consider your image down to the last detail, because your audience is making decision about you from the moment you rise up and stand before them. "So know how to dress well and be aware of self-image". For self image to dress well follows these simple rules.

- Do not be guided by fashion.

- Wear what suits you and is comfortable.

- Be aware to dress according to the audience and situation.

- Ensure that your image remain neat and clean.

IMAGE RULE FOR MEN

It is really important that you set the right tone from the start and wear clothes that make a strong first impression.

If you are wearing Jacket, the jacket button must be fastened. The closed jacket gives you a well-groomed appearance. Remember that the jacket must be neat and clean. Generally everyone wears a matching shirt. Ensure that your sleeves are not hidden by the jacket. Shirt sleeves should remain at least one inch beyond your jacket sleeves. If shirt fits well, shorten your jacket sleeves length. You can get it done from any experienced tailor. Ensure that following above rules your jacket should be comfortable. (i.e., neither too loose nor too tight)

Next proper attention must be paid to your trouser. Trouser must always be well fitted at your waist. Ensure that the fitting at waist is such that you do not need the assistance of your belt. If your trouser fits well you can use belt, but do not use belt to fit your trouser at waist. Trouser length must be measured by the professional and it should be at least two finger space above the top of your shoe heal, but not below. The leg width of your trouser should neither be too tight nor too loose.

When you are wearing Jacket and trouser, do not try to match their colors. Contrast colors are always better.

The color of your shirt should always match your Jacket. Collars of your shirt should not strangle you. There should be at least one finger space left when you have buttoned up. In informal wear, golf type shirt is often preferred.

The color of your tie should coordinate with your shirt. Ensure that it hangs up to the top of your belt, never beyond it. Many times people go for stylish shoes even if they may be pinching or uncomfortable. Keep it in mind that your feet carry the total weight of your body and if your shoes are not comfortable, you will waste your energy in discomfort. So ensure that your shoes are always comfortable. Make sure that they are polished sincerely. Always coordinate the color of your shoes with the color what you are wearing. Also coordinate the color and style of your socks with your shoes and clothes. Make sure that your socks stay up and do not fall in folds around your ankles. Do not wear white socks with black and brown shoes. Never wear white socks unless you are wearing white shoes. There are no such fixed rules for wearing accessories like watch, cufflinks etc.

IMAGE RULE FOR WOMEN

How long do you think take to impress the people on the other side (audience). For women it takes only 2-5 seconds to make first impression. Yes it also normally takes few second for the audience to judge if they want to listen to you sincerely or just listen. For women there are following three distinct elements responsible for their appearance or image.

- Clothing's, including appearance.

- Hygiene, hair, skin, nail care and make up.

- Body language, body posture, facial expression, manners and etiquette.

So the woman always wants to look sophisticated, well groomed and refined.

Shirt/Dress Length: It differs from women to women. It can be on the knee or below the knee which suits them. Find your shirt length by wearing the shirt and adjusting the length until your eyes tells you "Yes". Apply the same to shirt width. Accessories such as necklace, bracelet etc should match your dress. Let your accessories match your outfit not fight it. Do not wear heels that are too high, even if you are short. Shoes and hose/pajama should be coordinated and should enhance what you are wearing.

The women may need the advice of professional who can teach how to apply your make up so that you look natural and sophisticated. Make up enhance your look when it is well applied, but never over apply it. Women should make sure that their hair is clean and neat. If required you can go to the hairdresser before giving your presentation.

THINGS TO DO YOURSELF

The detail under each head has been explained. Every individual needs practice so that their image is unique to others. Remember your image is what is visible to others; hence it need top most priority.

Step - 9
Preparing The Script

WRITE TALK & READ TALK

WRITE TALK

Most people find it very difficult to write down the presentation you are going to deliver. The reason is very simple:- *"The way you speak is very different from the way you write."* When you write, you must follow the rules of grammar or else things won't make sense. But when you speak, you speak in more relaxed and easy manner. There are few tips which will help you to write your talk.

- Use short sentences. It is better to write two sentences instead of one long complicated sentence.

- Do not use big words that you would not use while talking to someone.

- You do not have to follow all the rules of written English grammar.

- Always read your speech aloud while you are writing it. You will observe right away if you sound like a book or a real person talking.

- Write talk must be repetitive. You should repeat salient point as many times as you want.

- Write talk must make use of questions. The asked questions can be direct, where you direct the question to a member in your audience or indirect question, which you answer yourself.

- Visual written aids- handouts, brochures, overheads, slides etc should be simple.

When you follow the rules of Write Talk, you will be astonished to know that how simple is scripting the presentation. You must remember the structure of the presentation and also should identify the type of your presentation you are going to give.

Visual Written Aids:- handouts, brochures, overheads, slides etc.

The only rule you have to remember about visual written aids is that they are always written in written style and not in Write Talk. The reason is that when you read directly from visual aids, it won't sound fluid to your audience. Another important thing is that whenever you read visual aids must be transcribed into Write Talk.. This means when you make reference to them, you are talking to your audience and not reading to them.

Keep your overheads, brochures and hand outs simple.

READ TALK

The greatest mistakes the presenters make is *reading*their script to the audience. Instead of delivering your presentation, you start reading your script; you can well imagine the reaction of the audience. No audience wants to be read to. If you read the script in such a way that it seems natural delivery to the audience, then there must be special method of scripting of your presentation. In other words, although you read your presentation, your audience impression is that you are talking to them. It is because that your read talk has been written in a way that you can look around for longer period, your pacing, pausing, eye contact and body language is complacent to your words.

Read Talk is a method of scripting your presentation in a format that is both easy to read and say. You will discover that once you start to write your script in Read Talk format, your delivery style will improve enormously. By following this format, you quickly find that you become so familiar with what is written and where it is written. You know exactly where to glance when you look down at your script. You will learn where to pause and ultimately you will start enjoying your presentation. There are certain rules to follow when transcribing your script into Read Talk, which are as follows.

- **Leave enough margin on either side:-** *'Eye can read text in the span about 6 degree of arc, which is wide enough to allow a clear view of about five words in a row when printed text at ordinary size is held 50 cm from the eyes.'* So make the width of your script matching span 6 degree of arc thereby leaving the margin of 1 ½ to 2 inch on either side. This way the script becomes much easier to scan and help you keep track of where you are. Now you practice it and become familiar with layout. Beside this the margin left on either side can be used for self instruction and to note where to insert slide.

Newspaper columns are the format which eye can scan at single glance.

- **Your script must be always double spaced:-** As the objective of the ReadTalk is to talk the script and not read it, the double spacing the script make it easier to follow than single space.

- **Use Upper and Lower Case:-** Upper and lower case is easier to read, because we are most familiar with this style of writing. Do not use italics or capitals. Remember the objective of the ReadTalk is to make your script both easy to read and talk, so it should be simple and familiar.

- **Separate the Paragraphs:-** Ensure to separate the paragraphs by at least four lines, so that script becomes clear in mind.

- **Complete the sentence on the same page:-**Do not end the sentence on the next page. Always end the sentence on the same page. The reason is that a sentence always ends with a natural pause. Use this to turn over the page.

- **Number each pages:-**This is essential and important. It can happen that your pages stick together and you accidently turn over two pages. By numbering pages you can avoid this.

- **Print your script in Blue:-** Do not use black color print. Blue color is easiest on the eyes, when you have to talk for long time, you may find your eyes become very tired, hence blue color.

EXERCISE ON Write Talk & Read Talk

WriteTalk
Topic: Your liberty of freedom

Good morning students.
Today I am going to defend our right and our liberty of freedom. Would you do something that you do not want, like smoking or drinking alcohol etc? Let me tell you that you are violating yourself as a person if your answer is yes, because you are doing things that can hurt, ruin and damage your body.

I am a high school student and am surrounded by peer students. They often tell you that if you drink alcohol you will get in to state of "happiness' and you will have a much better time.

Most kids are terrified that if they do not do this they will be alone, no friends and they will appear childish. Are they really your friends? They are not. They are misusing your freedom of thought.

Transcribing the WriteTalk into ReadTalk

Good morning/ students.

Today/ I am going to deliver/lecture on rights and our liberty/ of students./ Now let me know something/ that you do not want to do,/ like smoking or drinking alcohol ./ /

Let me tell you/ that you are violating yourself as a person/ if your answer is yes./ It is because you are hurting yourself/ and damaging your body /if you are doing these things.//

You are high school student/ and is surrounded by peers/ students./ They often tell you/ that if you drink alcohol/ you will get in to state of "happiness'/ and you will have a much better time.//

Most kids are terrified/ that if they do not do this/ they will be alone,/ no friends and they /will appear childish./ Now the question is ?/ Are they really your friends ? No / they are not. /They are misusing your/ freedom of thought.

ReadTalk

Good morning students.

Today I am going to deliver lecture

on rights and liberty of students.

Now let me know something

that you do not want to do,

like smoking or drinking alcohol .

Let me tell you that you are

Violating yourself as a person

if your   answer is yes.

It is because you are hurting yourself

and damaging your body

if you are doing these things.

You are high school student

and is surrounded by peers

students.

They often tell   you

that if you drink alcohol

you will get in to state of "happiness'

and you will have a much better time.

Most kids are terrified

that if they do not do this

they will be alone, no friends

and they will appear childish.

Now the question is ?

Are they really your friends ?

No they are not.

They are misusing your

Freedom of thought.

In the above WriteTalk the presentation norms such as structure, organize the presentation, message, font size etc has been kept in mind. And in the ReadTalk such as margin, double space script, separate paragraphs, short sentences and use of upper and lower case has been kept in mind. Now try to read the excerpt which is transcribed here into ReadTalk format. By following this format, you will quickly find that you become so familiar with what is written and where it is written that it almost seems as though you have memorized it. You know exactly where to glance when you look down at your script. You can practice it in front of mirror and you will observe how much easier it is to read ReadTalk than WriteTalk and you will discover that you start to enjoy giving presentation.

THINGS TO DO YOURSELF

- Take few paragraph from Newspaper article

- Convert into ReadTalk by transcribing

- Convert into ReadTalk format

- Practice in front of mirror

Step - 10
Delivering The Presentation

GETTING READY TO DELIVER

When you picked up this book, your apprehension was that this book is like mushrooms of books on the same subject in market, highlighting the negative aspect why you fail in delivering the expressive presentation or talk.

Now you are well on the road to accomplish what you wanted to do become you have now mentally prepared yourself by knowing your passion and inherent potential.

Now you can stand up confidently in front of your friends, peers or small group in gathering with your expressive voice.

Remember the script does not make a presentation. The presenter does it by his practice.

PRACTICE MAKES THE MAN PERFECT

The only way to strengthen your confidence and to feel free from any negative feeling is to practice. "Practice makes the man perfect", make this your motto. It is your decision to make. It is recommended that at the beginning you should write your script in full, in WriteTalk and than transcribe it into ReadTalk format and practice from this. Your aim is perfection—practice till you achieve.

The craftsman need years of practice to develop his skill. You can perfect your style of presentation almost immediately. Start now. Pick up a magazine or newspaper, take a few paragraphs from the article as WriteTalk and then transcribe it into ReadTalk format and practice it before the mirror.

By doing this you will master your own style, because the methods explained herein gives you the flexibility to do what is comfortable to you.

Step - 11
Salutation &
Greeting

NOW YOU CAN FACE ANYBODY

In the introduction I said that the presentation skill can be developed by anyone because of inherent potential. Now you have understood what you have to do, and what you have to practice. Because of your inherent potential you have learned how to talk, walk, ride a bicycle, play a sport and now you have to apply the same principle to learn the skill of presentation.

Any skill you have ever acquired follows

- First you have to understand the method,

- And then, with practice, you have to master the skill.

I have given you self propelled method **'THINGS TO DO YOURSELF'**. Now it's up to you. Practice! Practice! Practice! You can do it. With practice your self confidence will be boosted. If feel little cautious, start off small, go step by step. It doesn't matter if it takes you two months or two years. There is no time limit for personal growth. There is a saying that to cover a distance of 1000 km, you must take the first step. So start, because once you start, you will achieve what you want. Put all your energy into it.

Now love talking to people. If you have to give presentation, prepare according to structure, convert

WriteTalk to ReadTalk format, and practice and exercise for expressive voice and then deliver, I am sure you will succeed.

My salutation and greetings to you

www.ingramcontent.com/pod-product-compliance
Lightning Source LLC
LaVergne TN
LVHW050418160726
843469LV00041B/1122